A gift for

_____

From

_____

© 2012 by H. Jackson Brown Jr.

Life's Little Instruction Book is a registered trademark of
H. Jackson Brown Jr. www.instructionbook.com

Published in Nashville, Tennessee, by Thomas Nelson. Thomas
Nelson is a registered trademark of Thomas Nelson, Inc.

Thomas Nelson, Inc., titles may be purchased in bulk for
educational, business, fund-raising, or sales promotional
use. For information, please e-mail SpecialMarkets@
ThomasNelson.com.

ISBN 978-1-4003-1996-1

Printed in the United States of America

13 14 15 WOR 6 5 4

Life's Little Instruction Book®

H. Jackson Brown Jr.

THOMAS NELSON
Since 1798

NASHVILLE   DALLAS   MEXICO CITY   RIO DE JANEIRO

Introduction

This book began as a gift to my son, Adam. As he packed his stereo, typewriter, blue blazer, and other necessities for his new life as a college freshman, I retreated to the family room to jot down a few observations and words of counsel I thought he might find useful.

I read years ago that it was not the responsibility of parents to pave the road for their children, but to provide a road map. That's how I hoped he would use these mind-and-heart reflections.

I started writing, and what I thought would take a few hours took several days. I gathered my collection of handwritten notes, typed them up, and put them in a dime-store binder. I walked to the garage and slid it under the front seat of the station wagon.

A few days later his mother and I helped him move into his new dorm room. When he was all settled in, I asked him to come with me to the parking lot. It was time for the presentation. I reached under the car seat and, with words to the effect that this was what I knew about living a happy and rewarding life, handed him the bound pages. He hugged me and shook my hand. It was a very special moment.

Well, somehow those typewritten pages became the little book you're now holding. You may not agree with all the entries, and from your own life experience, I'm sure you could add hundreds more. Obviously, some are more important than others, but all have added a degree of joy, meaning, and efficiency to my life.

A few days after I had given Adam his copy, he called me from his dorm room. "Dad," he said, "I've been reading the instruction book, and I think it's one of the best gifts I've ever received. I'm going to add to it and someday give it to my son."

Every once in a while life hands you a moment so precious, so overwhelming you almost glow. I know. I had just experienced one.

H. J. B.

For Adam, my son and
in many ways my teacher.

Son, how can I help you see?
May I give you my shoulders to stand on?
Now you see farther than me.
Now you see for both of us.
Won't you tell me what you see?

1. Compliment three people every day.

2. Have a dog.

3. Watch a sunrise at least once a year.

4. Remember other people's birthdays.

5. Buy whatever kids are selling on card tables in their front yard.

6. Have a firm handshake.

7. Overtip breakfast waitresses.

8. Life is short. Eat more pancakes and fewer rice cakes.

9. Say "thank you" a lot.

10. Say "please" a lot.

11. Learn to play a musical instrument.

12. Sing in the shower.

13. Use the good silver.

14. Buy great books, even if you never read them.

15. Learn to make great chili.

16. Plant flowers every spring.

17. Be the first to say "hello."

18. Live beneath your means.

19. Drive inexpensive cars, but own the best house you can afford.

20. Be forgiving of yourself and others.

21. Learn the rules. Then break some.

22. Learn three
    clean jokes.

23. Wear polished shoes.

24. Floss your teeth.

25. Drink champagne
    for no reason at all.

26. Ask for a raise
    when you feel
    you've earned it.

27. If in a fight, hit
    first and hit hard.

28. Return all the
    things you borrow.

29. Teach some
kind of class.

30. Be a student in
some kind of class.

31. Never buy a house
without a fireplace.

32. Once in your life
own a convertible.

33. Plant a tree on
your birthday.

34. At meetings, resist
turning around to
see who has just
arrived late.

35. Donate two pints of blood every year.

36. Treat everyone you meet like you want to be treated.

37. Learn to identify the music of Chopin, Mozart, and Beethoven.

38. Make new friends but cherish the old ones.

39. Keep secrets.

40. Take lots of snapshots.

41. Never refuse
    homemade brownies.

42. Don't postpone joy.

43. Write thank-you
    notes promptly.

44. Show respect
    for teachers.

45. Show respect for
    police officers and
    firefighters.

46. Show respect for
    military personnel.

47. Never give up on anybody. Miracles happen every day.

48. Don't waste time
learning the "tricks
of the trade." Instead,
learn the trade.

49. Keep a tight rein
on your temper.

50. Buy vegetables from
truck farmers who
advertise with hand-
lettered signs.

51. Put the cap back
on the toothpaste.

52. Take out the garbage
without being told.

53. Avoid overexposure
to the sun.

54. Vote.

55. Surprise loved
ones with little
unexpected gifts.

56. Stop blaming others.
Take responsibility for
every area of your life.

57. Never mention
being on a diet.

58. Make the best of
bad situations.

59. Live so that when your children think of fairness, caring, and integrity, they think of you.

60. Support a high school band.

61. Admit your mistakes.

62. Ask someone to pick up your mail and daily paper when you're out of town. Those are the first two things potential burglars look for.

63. Use your wit to amuse, not abuse.

64. Remember that all news is biased.

65. Take a photography course.

66. Be brave. Even if you're not, pretend to be. No one can tell the difference.

67. Let people pull in front of you when you're stopped in traffic.

68. Always accept an outstretched hand.

69. Demand excellence and be willing to pay for it.

70. Whistle.

71. Give to charity all the clothes you haven't worn during the past three years.

72. Never forget your anniversary.

73 Never hire someone you wouldn't invite home to dinner.

74. Choose a charity in your community and support it generously with your time and money.

75. Never give up on what you really want to do. The person with big dreams is more powerful than one with all the facts.

76. Don't take good health for granted.

77. When someone wants to hire you, even if it's for a job you have little interest in, talk to them. Never close the door on an opportunity until you've had a chance to hear the offer in person.

78. Don't mess with drugs, and don't associate with those who do.

79. Slow dance.

80. Someone will always be looking at you as an example of how to behave. Don't disappoint.

81. Avoid sarcastic remarks.

82. Forget the Joneses.

83. Even if you're financially well-to-do, have your children earn and pay for *all* their automobile insurance.

84. Don't smoke.

85. When you want
    to teach a lesson,
    tell a story.

86. Even if you're
    financially well-to-do,
    have your children
    earn and pay part of
    their college tuition.

87. In business and in
    family relationships,
    remember that the
    most important
    thing is trust.

88. Refill ice cube trays.

89. Don't let anyone
    ever see you tipsy.

90. Become knowledgeable about antiques, oriental rugs, and contemporary art.

91. Recycle old newspapers, bottles, and cans.

92. Never invest more in the stock market than you can afford to lose.

93. Make it a habit to do nice things for people who'll never find out.

94. Attend class reunions.

95. Always have something beautiful in sight, even if it's just a daisy in a jelly glass.

96. Think big thoughts, but relish small pleasures.

97. Lend only those books you never care to see again.

98. Never start a business with someone who has more troubles than you.

99. Read the Bill of Rights.

100. Learn how to read a financial report.

101. Tell your kids often how terrific they are and that you trust them.

102. Never cheat.

103. Use credit cards only for convenience, never for credit.

104. Treat yourself to a massage on your birthday.

105. Take a brisk thirty-minute walk every day.

106. When dining with clients or business associates, never order more than one cocktail or one glass of wine. If no one else is drinking, don't drink at all.

107. Know how to drive a stick shift.

108. Spread crunchy peanut butter on Pepperidge Farm Gingerman cookies for the perfect late-night snack.

109. Smile a lot. It costs nothing and is beyond price.

110. Never use profanity.

111. Never argue with police officers, and address them as "officer."

112. Learn to identify local wildflowers, birds, and trees.

113. Keep a fire extinguisher in your kitchen and car.

114. Respect your children's privacy. Knock before entering their rooms.

115. Install dead bolts
on outside doors.

116. Don't buy expensive
wine, luggage,
or watches.

117. Consider writing
a living will.

118. Learn CPR.

119. Resist the temptation
to buy a boat.

120. Stop and read
historical roadside
markers.

121. Put a lot of little marshmallows in your hot chocolate.

122. Never buy something you don't need just because it's on sale.

123. Learn to listen. Opportunity sometimes knocks very softly.

124. Know how to change a tire.

125. Know how to tie a bow tie.

126. Wear audacious underwear under the most solemn business attire.

127. Leave the toilet seat in the down position.

128. Introduce yourself
to the manager
where you bank.
It's important that
he or she knows
you personally.

129. Learn the capitals
of the states.

130. Visit Washington,
D.C., and do the
tourist bit.

131. Have crooked teeth
straightened.

132. Have dull-colored
teeth whitened.

133. Be the first to forgive.

134. Never deprive someone of hope; it might be all they have.

135. When people are relating important events that happened to them, don't try to top them with a story of your own. Let them have the stage.

136. Keep your watch five minutes fast.

137. When starting out, don't worry about not having enough money. Limited funds are a blessing, not a curse. Nothing encourages creative thinking in quite the same way.

138. Pay your bills on time.

139. Don't buy cheap tools. Craftsman tools from Sears are among the best.

140. Give yourself an hour to cool off before responding to someone who has provoked you. If it involves something really important, give yourself overnight.

141. Join a slow-pitch softball league.

142. Sing in a choir.

143. Keep a flashlight and extra batteries under the bed and in the glove box of your car.

144. Take someone bowling.

145. Learn to handle a pistol and rifle safely.

146. Skip one meal a week and give what you would have spent to a homeless person.

147. When playing games with children, let them win.

148. Turn off the television
at dinnertime.

149. Get acquainted
with a good lawyer,
accountant, and
plumber.

150. Fly Old Glory on
the Fourth of July.

151. Stand at attention
and put your hand
over your heart
when singing the
national anthem,
and if wearing a
hat, remove it.

152. Talk slow
but think
quick.

153. Have a will and
tell your next of kin
where it is.

154. Have regular medical
and dental checkups.

155. Take time to
smell the roses.

156. Be tough minded
but tenderhearted.

157. Pray not for things,
but for wisdom
and courage.

158. Use seat belts.

159. Strive for excellence, not perfection.

160. Keep your desk and work area neat.

161. Take an overnight train trip and sleep in a Pullman.

162. Avoid negative people.

163. Resist telling people how something should be done. Instead, tell them *what* needs to be done. They will often surprise you with creative solutions.

164. Learn to make something beautiful with your hands.

165. Don't waste time
     responding to
     your critics.

166. Don't scrimp in
     order to leave money
     to your children.

167. Be original.

168. Be neat.

169. Be punctual and
     insist on it in others.

170. Be suspicious of
     all politicians.

171. Never take action
     when you're angry.

172. Encourage your children to have a part-time job after the age of sixteen.

173. Read carefully anything that requires your signature. Remember, the big print giveth and the small print taketh away.

174. Give people a second chance, but not a third.

175. When you're proud of your children, let them know it.

176. Be kinder than necessary.

177. Be your wife's best friend.

178. Do battle against prejudice and discrimination wherever you find it.

179. Wear out, don't rust out.

180. Be romantic.

181. Don't forget, a person's greatest emotional need is to feel appreciated.

182. Be insatiably curious. Ask "why" a lot.

183. Never criticize the person who signs your paycheck. If you are unhappy with your job, find another one.

184. Learn how to fix a leaky faucet and toilet.

185. Become the most positive and enthusiastic person you know.

186. Measure people by the size of their hearts, not the size of their bank accounts.

187. Let people know what you stand for—and what you won't stand for.

188. Don't worry if you can't give your kids the best of everything. Give them *your* very best.

189. Have good posture.
Enter a room
with purpose and
confidence.

190. Observe the
speed limit.

191. Drink low-fat milk.

192. Use less salt.

193. Eat less red meat.

194. Don't quit a job
until you've lined
up another.

195. Determine the quality of a neighborhood by the manners of the people living there.

196. Park at the back of the lot at shopping centers. The walk is good exercise.

197. Surprise a new neighbor with one of your favorite homemade dishes— and include the recipe.

198. Don't carry a grudge.

199. Look for
ways to make
your boss
look good.

200. Loosen up. Relax. Except for rare life-and-death matters, nothing is as important as it seems.

201. Don't watch violent television shows, and don't buy the products that sponsor them.

202. Show respect for all living things.

203. Return borrowed vehicles with the gas tank full.

204. Choose work that is in harmony with your values.

205. Swing for the fence.

206. Attend high school art shows, and always buy something.

207. Don't waste time grieving over past mistakes. Learn from them and move on.

208. Take your dog to obedience school. You'll both learn a lot.

209. Don't allow the phone to interrupt important moments. It's there for your convenience, not the caller's.

210. Give your best to your employer. It's one of the best investments you can make.

211. Commit yourself to constant self-improvement.

212. When complimented, a sincere "thank you" is the only response required.

213. Don't plan a long evening on a blind date. A lunch date is perfect. If things don't work out, both of you have wasted only an hour.

214. Don't discuss business in elevators or restrooms. You never know who may overhear you.

215. Have impeccable manners.

216. Be a good loser.

217. Be a good winner.

218. Never go grocery shopping when you're hungry. You'll buy too much.

219. Spend less time worrying who's right and more time deciding what's right.

220. Praise in public.

221. Criticize in private.

222. Don't major in minor things.

223. Think twice before burdening a friend with a secret.

224. Never tell anyone they look tired or depressed.

225. When someone hugs you, let them be the first to let go.

226. Never pay for work
     before it's completed.

227. Keep good company.

228. Keep a daily journal.

229. Keep your promises.

230. Teach your children
     the value of money
     and the importance
     of saving.

231. Don't be deceived by
     first impressions.

232. Resist giving advice concerning matrimony, finances, or hairstyles.

233. Remember the three Rs: respect for self; respect for others; responsibility for all your actions.

234. Seek out the good
in people.

235. Don't encourage
rude or inattentive
service by tipping the
standard amount.

236. Watch the movie
It's a Wonderful Life
every Christmas.

237. Respect tradition.

238. Drink eight glasses
of water every day.

239. Be cautious about lending money to a friend. You might lose both.

240. Never waste an opportunity to tell good employees how much they mean to the company.

241. Wave at children on school buses.

242. Buy a bird feeder and hang it so that you can see it from your kitchen window.

243. Never cut what can be untied.

244. Be modest.
A lot was
accomplished
before you
were born.

245. Make a video of your
     parents' memories
     of how they met
     and their first years
     of marriage.

246. Show respect for
     others' time. Call
     whenever you're
     going to be more than
     five minutes late for
     an appointment.

247. Hire people smarter
     than you.

248. Take good care of
     those you love.

249. Learn to show enthusiasm, even when you don't feel like it.

250. Keep it simple.

251. Never ask a lawyer or accountant for business advice. They are trained to find problems, not solutions.

252. Don't jaywalk.

253. Avoid like the plague any lawsuit.

254. Learn to show cheerfulness, even when you don't feel like it.

255. Take family vacations whether you can afford them or not. The memories will be priceless.

256. Be the first adult to jump into the pool or run into the ocean with the kids. They will love you for it.

257. When meeting people for the first time, resist asking what they do for a living. Enjoy their company without attaching any labels.

258. Don't gossip.

259. Don't discuss salaries.

260. Don't nag.

261. Don't gamble.

262. Don't whine.

263. Every day show
     your family
     how much you
     love them with
     your words,
     with your touch,
     and with your
     thoughtfulness.

264. Beware of the person who has nothing to lose.

265. Leave everything a little better than you found it.

266. Lie on your back and look at the stars.

267. Don't leave car keys in the ignition.

268. Arrive at work early and stay beyond quitting time.

269. When facing a difficult task, act as though it is impossible to fail. If you're going after Moby Dick, take along the tartar sauce.

270. Change air conditioner filters every three months.

271. Never overstay your welcome.

272. Fill your gas tank when it falls below one-quarter full.

273. Don't expect money to bring you happiness.

274. Never snap your fingers to get someone's attention. It's rude.

275. Remember that overnight success usually takes about fifteen years.

276. Promise big.

Deliver big.

277. No matter how
     dire the situation,
     keep your cool.

278. When paying cash,
     ask for a discount.

279. Don't use a toothpick
     in public.

280. Never underestimate
     your power to
     change yourself.

281. Never overestimate
     your power to
     change others.

282. Find a good tailor.

283. Practice empathy. Try to see things from other people's point of view.

284. Discipline yourself to save money. It's essential to success.

285. Get and stay in shape.

286. Find some other way of proving your manhood than by shooting defenseless animals and birds.

287. Remember, the deal's not done until the check has cleared the bank.

288. Don't burn bridges. You'll be surprised how many times you have to cross the same river.

289. Don't spread yourself
too thin. Learn
to say no politely
and quickly.

290. Keep overhead low.

291. Keep expectations
high.

292. Remember that a
successful marriage
depends on two
things: (1) finding the
right person and (2)
being the right person.

293. See problems as
opportunities
for growth and
self-mastery.

294. Accept pain and
disappointment
as part of life.

295. Compliment the meal
when you're a guest
in someone's home.

296. Make the bed
when you're an
overnight visitor in
someone's home.

297. Don't believe people when they ask you to be honest with them.

298. Judge your success by the degree that you're enjoying peace, health, and love.

299. Don't expect life to be fair.

300. Don't insist on running someone else's life.

301. Lock your car even if it's parked in your own driveway.

302. Never go to bed with dirty dishes in the sink.

303. Learn to handle a handsaw and a hammer.

304. Contribute five percent of your income to charity.

305. When tempted to criticize your parents, spouse, or children, bite your tongue.

306. Never underestimate the power of love.

307. Never underestimate the power of forgiveness.

308. Don't leave a ring in the bathtub.

309. Take a nap on Sunday afternoons.

310. Never buy dark-colored sheets or towels.

311. Don't bore people with your problems. When someone asks you how you feel, say, "Terrific, never better." When they ask, "How's business?" reply, "Excellent, and getting better every day."

312. Learn to disagree without being disagreeable.

313. Be tactful. Never
alienate anyone
on purpose.

314. Hear both sides
before judging.

315. Refrain from envy.
It's the source of
much unhappiness.

316. Be courteous
to everyone.

317. Wave to crosswalk
patrol mothers.

318. Remember that winners do what losers don't want to do.

319. Don't delay acting on a good idea. Chances are someone else has just thought of it too. Success comes to the one who acts first.

320. Don't say you don't have enough time. You have exactly the same number of hours per day that were given to Helen Keller, Louis Pasteur, Michelangelo, Mother Teresa, Leonardo da Vinci, Thomas Jefferson, and Albert Einstein.

321. When there's no time for a full workout, do push-ups.

322. Rekindle old friendships.

323. Instead of using the words *if only*, try substituting the words *next time*.

324. Instead of using the word *problem*, try substituting the word *opportunity*.

325. Every so often, push your luck.

326. Seek opportunity, not security. A boat in a harbor is safe, but in time its bottom rots out.

327. Live your life as an exclamation, not an explanation.

328. When traveling, put a card in your wallet with your name, home phone, the phone number of a friend or close relative, important medical information, plus the phone number of the hotel or motel where you're staying.

329. Try everything offered by supermarket food demonstrators.

330. When renting a car for a couple of days, splurge and get the one you would someday like to own.

331. Be wary of people
who tell you how
honest they are.

332. Install smoke detectors
in your home.

333. Get your next pet from
the animal shelter.

334. Live your life so that
your epitaph could
read, "No regrets."

335. Reread your
favorite book.

336. Be bold and courageous. When you look back on your life, you'll regret the things you didn't do more than the ones you did.

337. When you arrive at your job in the morning, let the first thing you say brighten everyone's day.

338. Never walk out on a quarrel with your wife.

339. Don't be fooled. If something sounds too good to be true, it probably is.

340. Regarding furniture and clothes: if you think you'll be using them five years or longer, buy the best you can afford.

341. Own a good
     dictionary.

342. Own a good thesaurus.

343. Go through all your
     old photographs.
     Select ten and tape
     them to your kitchen
     cabinets. Change them
     every thirty days.

344. Remember the three
     most important
     things when buying
     a home: location,
     location, location.

345. Keep valuable papers
in a bank lockbox.

346. Just for fun, attend a
small-town Fourth
of July celebration.

347. To explain a romantic
breakup, simply say,
"It was all my fault."

348. Be there when
people need you.

349. Evaluate yourself by
your own standards,
not someone else's.

350. Let your representatives in Washington know how you feel. Go to www .house.gov or www .senate.gov to get their contact information.

351. Be decisive even if it means you'll sometimes be wrong.

352. Don't let anyone talk you out of pursuing what you know to be a great idea.

353. Be prepared to lose once in a while.

354. Never waste an opportunity to tell someone you love them.

355. Never give loved ones a gift that suggests they need improvement.

.

356. Every day look for some small way to improve your marriage.

357. Every day look for some small way to improve the way you do your job.

358. Acquire things the old-fashioned way: save for them and pay cash.

359. Know when to keep silent.

360. Know when to speak up.

361. Remember, no one makes it alone. Have a grateful heart and be quick to acknowledge those who help you.

362. Do business with those who do business with you.

363. Just to see how it feels, for the next twenty-four hours refrain from criticizing anybody or anything.

364. Give your clients your enthusiastic best.

365. Work hard to create a good self-image in your children. It's the most important thing you can do to ensure their success.

366. Take charge of your attitude. Don't let someone else choose it for you.

367. Let your children overhear you saying complimentary things about them to other adults.

368. Save an evening a week for just you and your wife.

369. Carry jumper cables in your car.

370. Get all repair estimates in writing.

371. Pay attention to the details.

372. Be a self-starter.

373. Be loyal.

374. Forget committees. New, noble, world-changing ideas always come from one person working alone.

375. Never eat the last cookie.

376. Understand that happiness is not based on possessions, power, or prestige but on relationships with people you love and respect.

377. When undecided about what color to paint a room, choose antique white.

378. Carry stamps in your wallet. You never know when you'll discover the perfect card for a friend or loved one.

379. Compliment even
small improvements.

380. Turn off the tap when
brushing your teeth.

381. Wear expensive shoes,
belts, and ties, but
buy them on sale.

382. Start meetings on
time regardless of
who's missing.

383. Street musicians
are a treasure. Stop
for a moment and
listen; then leave a
small donation.

384. Don't ever watch
hot dogs or sausage
being made.

385. When faced with a
serious health problem,
get at least three
medical opinions.

386. Support equal pay
for equal work.

387. Pay your fair share.

388. Remain open,
flexible, and curious.

389. Never give anyone
a fruitcake.

390. Never acquire just one kitten. Two are a lot more fun and no more trouble.

391. Stay out of nightclubs.

392. Begin each day with your favorite music.

393. Visit your city's night court on a Saturday night.

394. When attending meetings, sit down front.

395. If you're going to be weird, be confident about it.

396. Focus on making things better, not bigger.

397. Don't be intimidated by doctors and nurses. Even when you're in the hospital, it's still your body.

398. Read hospital bills carefully. It's reported that 89 percent contain errors—in favor of the hospital.

399. Don't let your possessions possess you.

400. Wage war against littering.

401. Every once in a while, take the scenic route.

402. Don't procrastinate. Do what needs doing when it needs to be done.

403. Cut your own firewood.

404. After experiencing inferior service, food, or products, bring it to the attention of the person in charge. Good managers will appreciate knowing.

405. When you and your wife have a disagreement, regardless of who's wrong, apologize. Say, "I'm sorry I upset you. Would you forgive me?" These are healing, magical words.

406. Be enthusiastic about the success of others.

407. Don't flaunt your success, but don't apologize for it either.

408. Read to your children.

409. Sing to your children.

410. Listen to your children.

411. Get your priorities straight. No one ever said on his deathbed, "Gee, if I'd only spent more time at the office."

412. Don't allow self-pity. The moment this emotion strikes, do something nice for someone less fortunate than you.

413. Don't accept "good enough" as good enough.

414. Take care of your reputation. It's your most valuable asset.

415. Turn on your headlights when it begins to rain.

416. Select a doctor your own age so that you can grow old together.

417. Don't tailgate.

418. Sign and carry your organ donor card.

419. Share the credit.

420. Do more than is expected.

421. Go to a county fair and check out the 4-H Club exhibits. It will renew your faith in the younger generation.

422. Have a friend who owns a truck.

423. When a guest, don't let anyone see you go back more than twice for the peeled shrimp.

424. Enjoy real maple syrup.

425. At the movies, buy Junior Mints and sprinkle them on your popcorn.

426. Have some knowledge of three religions other than your own.

427. Make a list of ten things you want to experience before you die. Carry it in your wallet and refer to it often.

428. Answer the phone with enthusiasm and energy in your voice.

429. Every person you meet knows something you don't; learn from them.

430. Never put a candy
   dish next to the phone.

431. Record your
   parents' laughter.

432. When meeting people
   you don't know well,
   extend your hand
   and give them your
   name. Never assume
   they remember
   you even if you've
   met them before.

433. Do it right the
   first time.

434. Laugh a lot. A good sense of humor cures almost all of life's ills.

435. Don't rain on other people's parades.

436. Don't undertip the waiter just because the food is bad; he didn't cook it.

437. Change your car's oil and filter every three thousand miles regardless of what the owner's manual recommends.

438. Never underestimate the power of a kind word or deed.

439. Keep a notepad and pencil on your bedside table. Million-dollar ideas sometimes strike at 3 a.m.

440. Conduct family fire drills. Be sure everyone knows what to do in case the house catches fire.

441. Be open to new ideas.

442. Don't be afraid to say, "I don't know."

443. Don't be afraid to say, "I made a mistake."

444. Don't be afraid to say, "I need help."

445. Don't be afraid to say, "I'm sorry."

446. Show respect for everyone who works for a living, regardless of how trivial their job.

447. When you find a job that's ideal, take it regardless of the pay. If you've got what it takes, your salary will soon reflect your value to the company.

448. Send your loved one flowers. Think of a reason later.

449. Set short-term and long-term goals.

450. Attend your children's
athletic contests,
plays, and recitals.

451. Look for opportunities
to make people
feel important.

452. Never compromise
your integrity.

453. Stand when greeting a
visitor to your office.

454. Don't use time or
words carelessly.
Neither can be
retrieved.

455. Don't interrupt.

456. When a child falls
and skins a knee or
elbow, always show
concern; then take
the time to "kiss it
and make it well."

457. When talking to the
press, remember
they always have
the last word.

458. When planning a
trip abroad, read
about the places
you'll visit before
you go or, better yet,
rent a travel video.

459. Don't miss the magic of the moment by focusing on what's to come.

460. Improve your performance by improving your attitude.

461. Don't be rushed into making an important decision. People will understand if you say, "I'd like a little more time to think it over. Can I get back to you tomorrow?"

462. Before leaving to meet a flight, check first to be sure it's on time.

463. Be prepared. You never get a second chance to make a good first impression.

464. Give thanks before every meal.

465. Get into the habit of putting your billfold and car keys in the same place when entering your home.

466. Go the distance. When you accept a task, finish it.

467. Respond promptly to RSVP invitations. If there's a phone number, call; if not, write a note.

468. Never admit at work that you're tired, angry, or bored.

469. Don't expect others to listen to your advice and ignore your example.

470. Remember that enough is better than too much.

471. Learn a card trick.

472. Steer clear of restaurants that rotate.

473. Give people the benefit of the doubt.

474. Decide to get up thirty minutes earlier. Do this for a year, and you will add seven and one-half days to your waking world.

475. Patronize local merchants even if it costs a bit more.

476. Take a kid to the zoo.

477. Make someone's day
by paying the toll
for the person in the
car behind you.

478. Don't make the same
mistake twice.

479. Don't drive on
slick tires.

480. Save ten percent of
what you earn.

481. Never buy a beige car.

482. Watch for big problems. They disguise big opportunities.

483. Don't be called out on strikes. Go down swinging.

484. Keep an extra key hidden somewhere on your car in case you lock yourself out.

485. Never discuss money with people who have much more or much less than you.

486. Give yourself a year and read the Bible cover to cover.

487. Don't think a higher price always means higher quality.

488. Keep several irons
in the fire.

489. Cherish your children
for what they are,
not for what you'd
like them to be.

490. When negotiating
your salary, think
of what you want;
then ask for ten
percent more.

491. Be a leader.
Remember, the
lead sled dog is
the only one with
a decent view.

492. Question your goals by asking, "Will this help me become my very best?"

493. After you've worked hard to get what you want, take the time to enjoy it.

494. Be alert for
opportunities to
show praise and
appreciation.

495. Commit yourself
to quality.

496. Your mind can only
hold one thought
at a time. Make
it a positive and
constructive one.

497. Never underestimate
the power of words
to heal and reconcile
relationships.

498. Go home for
the holidays.

499. Count your blessings.

500. Never be too busy to
meet someone new.

501. Believe in love
at first sight.

502. Never laugh at
anyone's dreams.

503. Overpay good
babysitters.

504. Never refuse jury
duty. It is your civic
responsibility, and
you'll learn a lot.

505. Become someone's hero.

506. Love deeply and passionately. You might get hurt, but it's the only way to live life completely.

507. Carry Handi
     Wipes in your glove
     compartment.

508. Never apologize
     for being early for
     an appointment.

509. Open the car door for
     your wife, and always
     help her with her coat.

510. When reconvening
     after a conference
     break, choose a
     chair in a different
     part of the room.

511. Rake a big pile of
leaves every fall
and jump in it with
someone you love.

512. Don't judge people
by their relatives.

513. When you feel terrific,
notify your face.

514. Discipline with
a gentle hand.

515. Volunteer. Sometimes
the jobs no one
wants conceal big
opportunities.

516. Create a little signal only your wife knows so that you can show her you love her across a crowded room.

517. Never drive while holding a cup of hot coffee between your knees.

518. Never miss an opportunity to ride a roller coaster.

519. Never miss an opportunity to sleep on a screened-in porch.

520. Park next to the end curb in parking lots. Your car doors will have half the chance of getting dented.

521. Remember the advice of our friend Ken Beck: when you see a box turtle crossing the road, stop and put it safely on the other side.

522. When you go to borrow money, dress as if you have plenty of it.

523. Keep a diary of your accomplishments at work. Then when you ask for a raise, you'll have the information you need to back it up.

524. Never be the first to break a family tradition.

525. Never sign contracts with blank spaces.

526. In disagreements, fight fairly. No name-calling.

527. Put your address inside your luggage as well as on the outside.

528. Seize every opportunity for additional training in your job.

529. Accept a breath mint if someone offers you one.

530. Remember that everyone you meet is afraid of something, loves something, and has lost something.

531. Eat a piece of chocolate to cure bad breath from onions or garlic.

532. Check hotel bills carefully for unexpected charges.

533. Resist the temptation to put a cute message on your voice mail.

534. When someone asks you a question you don't want to answer, smile and ask, "Why do you want to know?"

535. Don't admire people
for their wealth
but for the creative
and generous ways
they put it to use.

536. Tour the main branch
of the public library
on Fifth Avenue the
next time you are
in New York City.
Unforgettable.

537. Never leave the
kitchen when
something's boiling
on the stove.

538. Never betray a
confidence.

539. Never claim a victory
prematurely.

540. Say "bless you"
when you hear
someone sneeze.

541. Don't let your family
get so busy that you
don't sit down to
at least one meal
a day together.

542. Make the punishment
fit the crime.

543. Remember that just the moment you say, "I give up," someone else seeing the same situation is saying, "My, what a great opportunity."

544. Be willing to lose a battle in order to win the war.

545. Take along a small gift for the host or hostess when you're a dinner guest. A book is a good choice.

546. When you lose, don't lose the lesson.

547. Don't overlook life's small joys while searching for the big ones.

548. Plant zucchini
only if you have
lots of friends.

549. Keep a well-stocked
first-aid kit in your
car and at home.

550. Order a seed catalog.
Read it on the day of
the first snowfall.

551. Don't let a little
dispute injure a
great friendship.

552. Ask your boss who
his or her heroes are.

553. When lost or in distress, signal in "threes"—three shouts, three gunshots, or three horn blasts.

554. Don't expect your love alone to make a neat person out of a messy one.

555. Every so often, invite the person in line behind you to go ahead of you.

556. Carry a small pocketknife.

557. Don't be surprised to discover that luck favors those who are prepared.

558. Remember that the person who steals an egg will steal a chicken.

559. Meet regularly with someone who holds vastly different views than you.

560. Be the first to fight for a just cause.

561. Remember that no time spent with your children is ever wasted.

562. Remember that no time is ever wasted that makes two people better friends.

563. Avoid approaching horses and restaurants from the rear.

564. Never say anything uncomplimentary about another person's dog.

565. Think twice before accepting the lowest bid.

566. Write a short note inside the front cover when giving a book as a gift.

567. Give people more than they expect, and do it cheerfully.

568. Make the rules for your children clear, fair, and consistent.

569. Memorize your favorite love poem.

570. Don't think expensive equipment will make up for lack of talent or practice.

571. Learn to say "I love you" in French, Italian, and Swedish.

572. Be ruthlessly realistic when it comes to your finances.

573. When you are totally exhausted but have to keep going, wash your face and hands and put on clean socks and a clean shirt. You will feel remarkably refreshed.

574. Make allowances for your friends' imperfections as readily as you do for your own.

575. When you realize you've made a mistake, take immediate steps to correct it.

576. Never miss a chance to dance with your wife.

577. Do your homework and know your facts, but remember, it's passion that persuades.

578. Smile when answering
the phone. The
caller will hear it
in your voice.

579. Don't waste time
trying to appreciate
music you dislike.
Spend the time with
music you love.

580. Set aside your dreams
for your children
and help them attain
their own dreams.

581. Dress a little better
than your clients
but not as well
as your boss.

582. Always put something in the collection plate.

583. Do the right thing, regardless of what others think.

584. Wear a shirt and tie to job interviews, even for a job unloading boxcars.

585. Take the stairs when it's four flights or less.

586. Never threaten if you don't intend to back it up.

587. Exercise caution the first day you buy a chain saw. You'll be tempted to cut down everything in the neighborhood.

588. Life will sometimes hand you a magical moment. Savor it.

589. Buy a used car with the same caution a naked man uses to climb a barbed-wire fence.

590. Don't confuse comfort with happiness.

591. Don't confuse wealth with success.

592. Remember people's names.

593. Make a habit of reading something inspiring and cheerful just before going to bed.

594. Marry a woman you love to talk to. As you get older, her conversational skills will be as important as any other.

595. Don't cut corners.

596. Never wash a car, mow a yard, or select a Christmas tree after dark.

597. Don't stop the parade to pick up a dime.

598. Turn enemies
into friends by
doing something
nice for them.

599. Remember that a
person who is foolish
with money is foolish
in other ways too.

600. Everyone loves praise.
Look hard for ways
to give it to them.

601. Be an original. If that
means being a little
eccentric, so be it.

602. Spend some
time alone.

603. Everybody deserves
a birthday cake.
Never celebrate a
birthday without one.

604. When it comes to
worrying or painting
a picture, know
when to stop.

605. Don't expect anyone
to know what you
want for Christmas if
you don't tell them.

606. Spend your time and energy creating, not criticizing.

607. Open your arms to change, but don't let go of your values.

608. Be as friendly to
the janitor as you
are to the chairman
of the board.

609. Mind your own
business.

610. When taking a woman
home, make sure she's
safely inside her house
before you leave.

611. Live with your new
pet several days
before you name
it. The right name
will come to you.

612. Every year celebrate
the day you and
your wife had
your first date.

613. Don't dismiss a
good idea simply
because you don't
like the source.

614. Be quick to take
advantage of an
advantage.

615. Slow down. I mean
really slow down
in school zones.

616. Allow your children to face the consequences of their actions.

617. When a good man or woman runs for political office, support him or her with your time and money.

618. When you need professional advice, get it from professionals, not from your friends.

619. Pay for a poor child to go to summer camp.

620. Choose a church that sings joyful music.

621. Don't waste time waiting for inspiration. Begin, and inspiration will find you.

622. Remember that silence is sometimes the best answer.

623. Be engaged at least six months before you get married.

624. When you say, "I'm sorry," look the person in the eye.

625. Spoil your wife, not your children.

626. Don't believe all you hear, spend all you have, or sleep all you want.

627. Win without boasting.

628. Lose without excuses.

629. When you find someone doing small things well, put him or her in charge of bigger things.

630. Deadlines are important. Meet them.

631. When opportunity knocks, invite it to stay for dinner.

632. Buy ladders, extension cords, and garden hoses longer than you think you'll need.

633. Don't confuse mere inconveniences with real problems.

634. Hold your child's hand every chance you get. The time will come all too soon when he or she won't let you.

635. Remember that the more you know, the less you fear.

636. Become your children's best teacher and coach.

637. When you carve the Thanksgiving turkey, give the first piece to the person who prepared it.

638. Learn to juggle.

639. Keep your private thoughts private.

640. Put your jacket around your girlfriend's shoulders on a chilly evening.

641. Be humble and polite,
     but don't let anyone
     push you around.

642. Put the strap around
     your neck before
     looking through
     binoculars.

643. Do 100 push-ups
     every day: 50 in
     the morning and
     50 in the evening.

644. Trust in God, but
     lock your car.

645. Get involved at your
     child's school.

646. Every so often let your spirit of adventure triumph over your good sense.

647. Use a favorite picture of a loved one as a bookmark.

648. On each of their
birthdays, give
your children a
hardback copy of
one of the classics.

649. Never lose your
nerve, your temper,
or your car keys.

650. Surprise an old friend
with a phone call.

651. Champion your wife.
Be her best friend
and biggest fan.

652. Apologize
immediately when
you lose your temper,
especially to children.

653. Mind the store. No one cares about your business the way you do.

654. Before going to bed on Christmas Eve, join hands with your family and sing "Silent Night."

655. Don't say no until you've heard the whole story.

656. Never put the car in drive until all passengers have buckled up.

657. Send your mother-
in-law flowers on
your wife's birthday.

658. Write your favorite
author a note of
appreciation.

659. When you know that
someone has gone to
a lot of trouble to get
dressed up, tell them
they look terrific!

660. Don't let weeds grow
around your dreams.

661. Read between
the lines.

662. Buy your fiancée
the nicest diamond
engagement ring
you can afford.

663. Don't be so concerned
with your rights
that you forget
your manners.

664. Remember that
almost everything
looks better after a
good night's sleep.

665. Remember that *how*
you say something
is as important as
what you say.

666. Be gentle with
the earth.

667. Leave a quarter where
a child can find it.

668. Stop and watch
stonemasons at work.

669. When you see visitors
taking pictures of
each other, offer
to take a picture of
them together.

670. Don't think you can
fill an emptiness
in your heart
with money.

671. Share your knowledge. It's a way to achieve immortality.

672. Never apologize for extreme measures when defending your values, your health, or your family's safety.

673. Buy a new tie to wear to your wedding rehearsal dinner. Wear it only once. Keep it forever.

674. When you're lost, admit it, and ask for directions.

675. Don't take good friends, good health, or a good marriage for granted.

676. Do a good job because you want to, not because you have to. This puts you in charge instead of your boss.

677. Keep impeccable tax records.

678. Bake bread with someone you love.

679. Start every day with the most important thing you have to do. Save the less important tasks for later.

680. When there is a hill to climb, don't think that waiting will make it smaller.

681. Pray. There is immeasurable power in it.

682. Remember that ignorance is expensive.

683. Help a child plant a small garden.

684. Hug children after you discipline them.

685. Once a year, go someplace you've never been before.

686. Spend your life lifting people up, not putting people down.

687. Remember that
     great love and
     great achievements
     involve great risk.

688. Don't trust a woman
     who doesn't close her
     eyes when you kiss her.

689. Brush your teeth
     before putting
     on your tie.

690. Remember that not
     getting what you
     want is sometimes a
     stroke of good luck.

691. Root for the
     home team.

692. Never interrupt when you're being flattered.

693. Never tell a person
who's experiencing
deep sorrow, "I
know how you
feel." You don't.

694. Ride a bike.

695. Never ignore evil.

696. Look people in the eye.

697. Be wary of the
man who's "all hat
and no cattle."

698. When there's a piano
to be moved, don't
reach for the stool.

699. Steer clear of restaurants with strolling musicians.

700. Go on blind dates.

701. Follow your own star.

702. Remember the ones who love you.

703. Marry only for love.

704. Don't get too big for your britches.

705. Call your mom and dad.